Before Fort Clatsop

poems by

Michelle Bonczek Evory

Finishing Line Press
Georgetown, Kentucky

Before Fort Clatsop

for all the brave who venture

Copyright © 2017 by Michelle Bonczek Evory
ISBN 978-1-63534-234-5 First Edition
All rights reserved under International and Pan-American Copyright Conventions. No part of this book may be reproduced in any manner whatsoever without written permission from the publisher, except in the case of brief quotations embodied in critical articles and reviews.

ACKNOWLEDGMENTS

Camas: "In Shoshoni"
Colonus Publishing: "On Melancholy, Meriwether Lewis, September 10, 1803," Spirit Mound, Meriwether Lewis, August 25, 1804," "Premonition at West Stone Creek, 1804," "On Chastity," "On the Nature of Females"
Connotations Press: "In Hidatsa"
Digital Americana: "American Baptism: The Birth of Sacagawea, circa 1789"
Orion Magazine: "Before Fort Clatsop, November 24, 1805"
Poetry Kanto: "The First Ship"
Slipstream: "Love Poem via Geyser"
Town Creek Poetry: "On Attraction"
Weber: The Contemporary West: "Yaquina Bay, and Darkness" and "Final Hike"

Milbrodt, Teresa, ed. *Manifest West: Contemporary Cowboy.* "Chico Hot Springs Saloon, MT." Gunnison: Western P Books, 2014.

"Yaquina Bay, and Darkness" is the recipient of the 2011 Sherwin W. Howard Award through *Weber: The Contemporary West*.

Several of these poems are the recipient of the 2016 Colonus Poetry Award.

Publisher: Leah Maines

Editor: Christen Kincaid

Cover Art: "View, Yellowstone" by Judy Dater, photographer (American, born 1941); from The Getty Public Domain database,
http://www.getty.edu/museum/media/images/web/enlarge/30819201.jpg

Author Photo: Rob Evory

Cover Design: Elizabeth Maines McCleavy

Printed in the USA on acid-free paper.
Order online: www.finishinglinepress.com
also available on amazon.com

Author inquiries and mail orders:
Finishing Line Press
P. O. Box 1626
Georgetown, Kentucky 40324
U. S. A.

Table of Contents

The First Ship 1
Chico Hot Springs Saloon, MT 2
American Baptism: The Birth of Sacagawea, circa 1789 4
In Shoshoni 5
In Hidatsa 6
Yaquina Bay, and Darkness 7
On Melancholy, Meriwether Lewis, September 10, 1803 9
Spirit Mound, Meriwether Lewis, August 25, 1804 10
Premonition at West Stone Creek, 1804 11
Revisiting the Dixon Bar 13
His Mother's Broth 15
On Attraction 16
On Blindness 17
On the Nature of Females 18
On Chastity 19
Final Hike 20
Before Fort Clatsop, November 24, 1805 22
Love Poem Via Geyser 23

Michelle Bonczek Evory's *Before Fort Clatsop* is fascinating contrapuntal poetry that counterpoints uniquely American themes with the universal. Each poem is set within a quilt-like patchwork of contrast that is framed within the universal theme of the quest. The quest is thematic to every culture, and it is engaged in by a hero. It is the stuff of mythological road trips—Odysseus yearning for home, Jason seeking his fleece, Frodo pursuing his ring. It is a staple of American literature—Mark Twain with his *Roughing It*, John Steinbeck with his *Travels with Charley*, Jack Kerouac with his *On the Road*.

The Great Explorers, those questers of the landscape of the Age of Discovery—Columbus, Magellan, Cortez, Pizarro, de Gama, Balboa, Cabot, Raleigh, Winthrop—had one thing in common: they were all males. Within the confines of our traditional western patriarchal culture, even if you were an Isabella or an Elizabeth, even if you were queen with powers of majesty and execution, if you wanted someone to find a new world, sale around it, conquer Mexico or Peru, take a gander at the Pacific or India, found colonies like Roanoke or Massachusetts Bay—you got yourself a man.

Every symbol is a particular that mouths on the universal. Meriwether Lewis and his Expedition are symbols of the male quest—a classic of discovery, of obtaining the goal of Land's End. Lewis's viewing of the Pacific is from the terminus of our Manifest Destiny as a nation. But Lewis's view from Fort Clatsop on the Oregon coast is a male's view—our national destiny is one of masculinity.

Sacagawea was a Shoshone of Idaho's Snake River Plain who had been captured as a girl by the Hidatsa, Sioux Indians who sold her to a French trapper in North Dakota. The Expedition for her was not one to Land's End as it was for Lewis; it was, rather, a returning home to family.

The stories of Lewis and Sacagawea that Michelle Bonczek Evory weaves into her poetic quilt are contrasting patches that recognize the counterpoint femininity plays to masculinity. In *Before Fort Clatsop* Bonczek Evory creates a valence of male and female that transcends sexual identity and speaks to universal humanity. Whether home is Ithaca or the Snake River Plain, the human emotion, that yearning for return, is in Bonczek Evory's quilt the same quest for man or woman.

But in the patriarchal western tradition of sky gods throwing male spears of lightning bolts, what exactly is the woman's quest if not Medea's cooking up her children in a vengeful stew to serve her Argonaut husband? Our fairy tales of Cinderella and Sleeping Beauty and Snow White are nothing but stories of male rescue. Can you envision Jane Austen writing anything that approximates *Fear and Loathing in Las Vegas: A Savage Journey to the Heart of the American Dream*? Is not the quintessential female quester of American Literature our Dorothy of fantasy searching for her home in Kansas?

In Sacagawea, Bonczek Evory has given us a Dorothy in the flesh searching for the Snake River, a woman chosen for her ability to communicate where the men could not. Lewis knew that in order to obtain Balboa's prize he would have to pass through the landscape of the Shoshone, and that without their help, without Sacagawea's help, he would fail. It is the woman in Bonczek Evory's quilt who by her power over language has the ultimate power over male destiny, and because of this the male's quest for the golden fleece of Land's End must be intertwined with the woman's quest for home and family.

The dedication in Bonczek Evory's chapbook is "for all the brave who venture." She utilizes the landscape of American history to make deft cross-cultural contrasts between native and American Anglo-Saxon culture. She makes acute observations in Montana bars showing that although culture develops and shifts in time, it remains undergirded by the commonality of basic human emotions. Bonczek Evory's work is a nuanced pattern of specifics—patches in a poetic quilt that sound in American experience. But there is a universality that underlies the contrapuntal patchwork of journeys she is evoking through culture and time when the quilt is viewed from the distance as a whole.

Her twenty-one poems begin with a patch in the quilt to show us a first ship, pass deftly through patches of native landscapes, burial mounds, bars in Montana, and the foreshadowing of Lewis's death by suicide or murder. Bonczek Evory stitches in a recognition of the position that American poetry has in the western tradition with five formal "On" poems that nod to Lucretius's *On the Nature of Things* and Milton's "On His Blindness." The quilt resolves itself in the "Love Poem Via Geyser" that suggests that love is both the end and the beginning of our journey, and whether we are male or female, it is our shared life cycle of ankles turned and healed again and of our shared splendor of living in the rain that makes us whole and human.

Bonczek Evory's poems end magnificently in a kiss. And what is a kiss but the ultimate resolution of human experience, that brush of cherry blossoms that drew Basho on the narrow road to the deep north?

Rich Skalstad,
author of *Fudge Day* and *Lawyers in Love*

The First Ship

      The first change came in the clouds, light, as if heaven
opened to take us in. But we were not taken in.
      After we came ashore, our children wept
as we took our first steps into the dark woods and,
      so many vines, so many lines of thorns. The men
cut them back with swords. They cut through
      inch by inch until we found a field wet with dusk.
We gathered pieces of that dark forest
      for fire, flames rising high as one woman began
to hum a hymn we'd never heard and my feet, possessed
      by a power not my own, began to move.
We slept little that first night, dreamed strange shapes
      and pulsing shadows of unknown animals, our hearts
loosed like husks fallen to earth.

Chico Hot Springs Saloon, MT

I'm tempted to call it
Yellowstone's crown, how it sits
above the park, just after

sharpened roadside cliffs and wild
mountain sheep nibbling grass, a rustic
resort where women—young women,

the regulars, in pretty clothes sit
at high tables waiting
for men in cowboy boots to lift

their hands and guide them
to the dance floor.
The live band plays country,

the singer wears a silver cowboy hat
while the bassist, you can tell, wants
nothing but to play jazz.

The couples circle each other's bodies,
step with the music. It is so easy
to make up the story. One man

in tight blue jeans, sandy hair falling
far below his neckline, has a hard groove
and no form. He's the type of dancer

my father used to say would pull
a girl's arm from her socket.
He's all hip and swing, untempered

patter of boots. His partners dizzy
yet come back song after song for another
spin. One man, the gentleman, slightly

older, is a perfect square. His shoulders,
his hips, he holds the waist of his partner
like a strong wind. He looks into her

eyes and she glides anywhere
his motion takes her. And among
the girls, the middle-aged woman,

you can tell, gorgeous once, still
slim and energetic, laughing
in a leopard-skin-patterned shirt slipping

from her shoulder, claps her hands
to the music, slaps her thigh, dances alone
some songs, at the front of the floor.

American Baptism: The Birth of Sacagawea, 1789

Between seams of field and pine,
a Shoshone woman births a daughter
to the night. Steam rises from their skin

like prayers rising from a congregation
thousands of miles to the east. Wrapping
her in fur, the mother cradles

her baby and walks through woods
to the river, whose shallows spiral
like stars above their heads,

like questions around all new bodies.
Had she listened to her dreams,
she would have let the little girl go

with the current, let the Salmon take her
straight to the Great Waters without divide.
But the shadow of a bird moved her

like wind moves a cloud. Like how
a comet captured by sun's gravity
marks the sky, draws faraway eyes west

by the millions. Boinaiv's mother
cupped the river and washed her blood
from her daughter's hands.

In Shoshoni

The young girl would one day live with another name,
Sacajawea, "boat puller," without questioning her strength
on the rope, without knowing who or what she was

pulling. Over far hills, her brother ran the horses. On the air,
voices of women, scent of salmon drying in summer's heat.
The pine trees lifted their needles to the sky.

Boinaiv threw a stone into the river and watched ripples
widen. One day she would dive from a pirogue into rapids
to save all she could: rifle, blanket, gunpowder, symbols

written in a large book she could not read, a language
without sound. Boinaiv lowered her hand to the ground
and looped an S, a shape that reminded her

of a rattle snake, carving the slow, soft rustle of earth beneath
her fingers. The sand trembled, and she raised a snakeskin
from the river's bank. Its delicate white flakes changed

light into colors she'd seen beading her grandmother's neck.
She held the scales to her eye and looked through:
the world before her blurred and whitened.

In Hidatsa

In their language they called her
"bird woman," *Sacagawea*,

her brother's voice fading
Boinaiv into the night.

Her black hair was as long as this
night, galloping until sunrise

when she could for the first time see
this man's streaked face

who had taken her
hair around his wrist like a rope

and pulled her whole body
onto the back of his painted horse.

Had she been a bird, she would've
pecked his dark eyes like seeds.

Boinaiv! They rode too fast for her
to look back. She had to lean into

the heat of her enemy's body, spread
her legs around his horse, clasp

his waist, open her lungs to breathe
his stench. For many snows, each time

her new name called, she wished
she had let go, had let her body crash

to the grass like a moon, before
it, too, learned how to break

itself into darkness, and return.

Yaquina Bay, and Darkness

We have never been down this road: the ocean
a womb, if you can imagine that, and if you can't, just the ocean
pounding a March night black and blue, the lighthouse

at the end of the bay's arm beaming, ready,
metaphorically speaking, for delivery of
what we call the body

from what we call
the body—what we'll call here *our bodies*
from *our life together*—white glare, loose stone,
       the ocean—we fall into it all
blindly, everything—each word

that breaks free from our mouths, each word, that is, that breaks
our mouths, whether right or wrong, for richer or for poorer, each word
forming and forming and forming.

I fear this Pacific rising toward our feet and cringe at the sound
of the horn breaking night
with its wail, this night breaking us.

Every two minutes the horn calls the lost ashore, which feels like me,

which is surely us, out here
lost among tufts of beach grass like wild hair
over the world in which we've lost

the piece of driftwood we used to mark our path
back. Once, I halted, stilled my lungs
for the whisper I heard over my heart. I followed
the sound, sleeplessly, for days. So now

you know it's not good when I say let's stop
walking, let's sit on this log
in this fog, I could say, for as long as it takes to lift,

until the waves stop throwing themselves
against what we cannot see, that which we refuse

to see. I know I don't want to go any further.

Even Niagara Falls sounds like a sigh
from far enough away.

I don't want to go any further, I say.

You close your mouth—no, you, *close* your mouth, catch
whatever is left of us

not yet lost to this language.

On Melancholy, Meriwether Lewis, September 10, 1803

> *I first dug superficially in several parts of it, and came to collections of human bones…These were lying in the utmost confusion, some vertical, some oblique, some horizontal, and directed to every point of the compass, entangled and held together in clusters by the earth.*
> ~Thomas Jefferson, *Notes on the State of Virginia*

Jefferson told me how he dug to unearth an Indian warrior.
How all he uncovered were bones.

Hundreds of Indians, all their lives the layered chapters of a story
decomposing. I wanted to tell him: I, too, am a builder of mounds.

On my chest, the weight of ten thousand graves; within,
a spinning compass of directions. A buffalo herd

the size of the moon pounding dusty thunder into my heart.
I do not know if I can bear this journey. Do not know if I can be

pulled back to center. Friend, pray my voice speak
only in wonder and command, that the dark remain

quieter than silence, my footfalls appear
lighter than dust.

Spirit Mound, Meriwether Lewis, August 25, 1804

> *Augt. 25th Satturday 1804   Set out to Visit this mountain of evel Spirits, we Set out from the mouth of the White Stone Creek*
> ~Captain William Clark

Here, where devils haunt Native ground, some part of me
pulled. Some darkness taking shape in my throat, my mouth

dry as these plains. These thoughts hasty, a flickering haze.
Lock your arms tight to your ribs, let your chest crack

from the weight, the ache, the burn strikes hard
through my fingers. I could scratch through larch, bite

the skin of those tarnal pears, lash a thousand lazy men, slash
lines into my own flesh. All day yesterday, now, ever more

the same. A fiery, windy August, bison grazing away
the distance. See the storm of insects seeking safety

behind the mound, see the larger winged creatures,
quietly feasting upon them.

Premonition at West Stone Creek, 1804

> *That night, Mrs. Grinder, the innkeeper's wife, heard several shots. She later said she saw a wounded Lewis crawling around, begging for water, but was too afraid to help him. He died, apparently of bullet wounds to the head and abdomen, shortly before sunrise the next day.*
> ~Abigail Tucker, "Meriwether Lewis' Mysterious Death,"
> *Smithsonian Magazine*

I bent over to drink
                         and for one moment

    I could not see

my reflection,
                         only a red ribbon bit

    of sky and a bird, a bird

I felt graze my head
                         like a hot round.

    Around last night's fire

a painted man leaned in,
                         told me thousands of birds

    are drawn by evil

to the burial mound.
                         That these birds
    sense death.

I didn't believe him.
                         Now, mound at my back,

    wing flap echoing

down my canal

           and, my darker self,

I hear you call back.

Revisiting the Only Bar in Dixon
    after Richard Hugo

I'd been there years before. Large jars of brined
pig's feet, beet-stained eggs covered half

the bar. Hugo's poem hung beside the jukebox
stocked with Hank Williams and John Prine.

From a fridge shaped like a beer can, the bartender
slung cans of Rainer. But today, new owner Bud

points up at the new flat screen TV. *You all like
drizzle on your food? Like that guy in orange shoes?*

His wife Joanne slides a cassette of 1940's swing
into the deck, shows us pictures of her

large Mormon family, tells us how Bud's mom left
Bud the bar in her will, how neighbors tried to kill

Bud's horses with hot dogs filled with antifreeze,
how she'd been in love with Bud, like all of her friends,

as a girl. Later, Joanne will slam her fist, raise
her voice when we mention Hugo. *He wronged*

Bud's mom! And from the drawer she'll pull
a crinkled, whiskey-stained sheet: "The Dixon Bar,

the only poetry heritage site in Montana," tell us
the bar's for sale. In an old electric skillet, Bud will fry

his secret recipe chicken, tell us the trick to good food
is to never clean the grill. He'll press his calloused

hands against my bare back to diagram cuts of meat,
tell us after even more scotch *You're too young to have anything*

worthwhile to say. And we'll let him, for the story. But right now, we're *kids* come up through Missoula

from the east to read poetry at the *"Hugo bar."*
Like we give a shit.

Montana, they tell us, *has a New York problem.*
Still, they warn us about the river folk, invite us

to pitch a tent in their lawn, pop open can after can
of Coors. And before the door closes, Joann will place

Bud's chicken wrapped in foil, warmly, in my hand,
along with a couple of cold, loose cans for the road.

His Mother's Broth

The men kept thick strips of salted deer, blocks
of dry broth that when reconstituted tasted

like their sweat. But at home in Virginia, his mom
would slide onion into stock, parsley bright green

as daffodil shoots. She'd let Meriwether
spoon soup into her mouth when he was a child

learning to balance, discovering how to hold still
his shaky hand, already knowing somehow

to blow gently over the spoon, his breath
making ripples on the broth's warm skin.

He remembered then the softened beets like roses
in her garden, the carrots broken into bite-sized pieces

like an evening rain, and the slivered leaves of basil,
summer itself a guest at their morning table.

While others guzzled broth from cups around the fire,
Meriwether stared quietly into the steam: fog lifting

off their pond, the graceful white neck
of his mother sitting beside him.

On Attraction

Meriwether spent nights imagining
the two of them at the pond, wrists submerged in dark
water, algae bright as April basil, mud slathering
ankle bones. With his brother Rueben he'd caught
salamanders and frogs when they were both little
and now he wanted to share the good
sliminess with Lydia, too, the rush, the thrill
of the grab, fat yellow of a frog so big you
need two hands to nab it, have to sneak
up quick from behind. Lydia squirmed, shrieked
beneath Meriwether as he shoved
the bullfrog's jeweled eyes to her face. He loved
how the ends of her hair dripped down her kerchief
how her loosened braids smelled of earth.

On Blindness

The blind priest Waddell would pace around Meriwether, nodding
in rhythm to conjugations: to covet: *cupio, cupivi, cupitus,
cupere*. Hundreds of miles away, Meriwether's mother, like a bird,

breaks a peach's flesh with her teeth, shapes a bite tiny
for his sister Jane's hands. To capture: *capio, cepi, captus,
capere*. She lifts the meat to her daughter's mouth, rubs

each lip with nectar. Jane shakes her head, puckers
at its sour sweetness, takes the slippery morsel with her tongue.
Meriwether stares into the woods, dreaming of Lydia, bringing her

a sack of peaches, fruit ripe, skin on the edge of bursting.
When she bites in, the wet rinses her chin and Meriwether catches
the sticky sugar with his thumb, brings down his tongue…

Instead, in Waddel's kitchen window, five softening peaches
sweeten the air. Meriwether closes his eyes rubbing hair
newly grown over his lower belly. He slips his fingers under his belt,

grip firm, a shaft of sunlight pulling behind the corner of the abbey,
away from the window where Waddell, bent over a bowl of peaches,
closes his eyes, breathes in the bruised fruit.

On the Nature of Females

She complained about the wet, the steep,
the divots. We had intended to stay the day,
watch the bursting summer sun seep
into western mountains. She complained
about her fear of heights, ticks, the slipperiness
beneath her slippers. She said she was cold—
it was July! I purposefully left my gun at the nest
heeding a friend's advice: *give the girl whole
attention.* But she went on about her sister, swooned
when I picked up, cut open a dead raccoon
so I'd better trap. We should've just left, but lavender
against my thighs, and that full moon floating further
up in the eastern sky, and Heather, rare as chenille,
so sweet on my tongue, if she could just hold hers still.

On Chastity

Over the rumbling waves of his men's
whiskey-strained snores, it was the girl
in small blue beads, he was sure, her moaning
from a nearby tent. Earlier beside the fire
she had ran her soft fingers across his cheek,
leaned into his ear. He did not understand her
language but her voice. Bell. Finch. Creek
bed beside his Georgia home. If he'd done more
than shake her off with a nod, wasn't so damn
shy, see, he'd rub his thumb over her lips. Apple jam.
Honeysuckle. Sweet peach. He was captain.
What would his men think? To give in to a woman,
he might've lost himself in her warmth, her kiss,
he might've finally discovered happiness.

Final Hike

We are exhausted.

The sun going down
on the Yellowstone gateway

one last time
before we can no longer turn
our heads and see it there

its July skies frisky with lightning
and hail, its wind so strong
it blows our eyes open:

white snow on Mt. Holmes
Mt. Bunsen's crumbling stones
otters slinking and tumbling

like individual whirlpools
in Trout Lake. The last family
poses for a picture

in front of the sign, the last bear
bumbles across a distant field.
We are so tired

of hot springs, we've passed
on Mammoth, our feet sockless
and sweaty, blistered red

from Specimen Ridge where we sat
on the edge of a fossilized redwood
accomplished and cursing

the hard path we planned on giving
three hours that took us six.
On the way down we opted

for meadow, divot
and hole threatening our ankles,
rather than sliding down

risky stripped paths.
We followed bent grass
left by elk and bison, crawling

on all fours, the wild
flowers dusting our skin
with their pollen.

Before Fort Clatsop, November 24, 1805

There are shadows a flag casts, and places
that shadow does not reach. This stretch of beach
kept sacred by winds and winter

and the hands that reach down to it,
discovers the waves by their crashing, the ice
by its cracking, the human voice by its wail

and song. This is a land of edges,
worn away stone. Here, we long
for that other shore that pulls like thread

through broken skin and sore muscle.
If we follow the river it takes us back
to a world of salmon and root.

If we stay we will be beaten by weather,
but there will be salt. What is it that leads us
always to the mouth?

It is so quiet I hear shells shake beneath my feet.
I wake from sleep and there is fur growing over my bones.
Lay your head on my shoulder.

Tomorrow we will all decide. For now,
we restless paw at each other, imagine dust
and sunlight and a land that echoes us back.

Love Poem via Geyser

Since we left Yellowstone, steam's risen
in hot clouds from the earth's cracked lips.
Bison have stood, smashing grass for tourists
whose cameras rise to their eyes, whose cars
brake and park on roadsides to view black bears
slurping down elk intestines. The fish we caught
and released lay eggs and fell for other lures.
My ankle I overturned in a ground-squirrel hole
has healed and turned again. Like the old tree we saw
suddenly fall to earth, split from its white trunk in old age,
others have fallen, too. My grandmother has died.
My parents have aged. Still, we have no children.
We've sang songs, drank wine, built fires, swam
in pools sailing the Mediterranean. Our bodies
rocked by the sea. Rocked by each other. We've married,
we've flown to Barcelona, Venice, Lisbon, Seattle.
You've driven to Boston alone and between Syracuse
and Annville more times than we counted. I've dreamt
about angels, your parents and mine. We've grown
gardens, eaten their fruits, shared the splendor of being
alive in rain, in sun. The moon waxed, waned,
eclipsed. The winters stormed, basements flooded.
We've cleaned our bodies and dirtied our feet. Walked
the sidewalks of so many cities in so many countries imagining
them all our home. How many miles have we run?
How many eggs have we eaten? We raised four hens, almost
slaughtered one rooster. I've said your name over and over
until my tongue's shape changed, until the droplets emerged
from my skin and evaporated in your mouth.

Michelle Bonczek Evory is the author of *The Art of the Nipple* (Orange Monkey Publishing, 2013) and the forthcoming Open SUNY Textbook *Naming the Unnameable: An Approach to Poetry for New Generations*. Her poetry is featured in the 2013 Best New Poets Anthology and has been published in over seventy journals and magazines, including *Crazyhorse, cream city review, Green Mountains Review, Orion Magazine,* and *The Progressive*. She holds a PhD from Western Michigan University, an MFA from Eastern Washington University, and an MA from SUNY Brockport. In 2015, she and her husband poet Rob Evory were the inaugural Artists in Residence at Gettysburg National Military Park. She teaches writing and literature in Kalamazoo, MI, and mentors poets at The Poet's Billow (thepoetsbillow.com).

www.ingramcontent.com/pod-product-compliance
Lightning Source LLC
LaVergne TN
LVHW021123080426
835510LV00021B/3303

www.ingramcontent.com/pod-product-compliance
Lightning Source LLC
LaVergne TN
LVHW021718080426
835510LV00010B/1028